Cyber Security Supplier Assurance

About the Author

A seasoned expert in the realm of cybersecurity, the author brings a unique blend of military discipline and industry insight to the forefront of their work. With over two decades of dedicated experience in Communications and IT—both in the UK's Armed Forces and the private sector—the author is well-equipped to tackle the intricacies of digital security. Their profound understanding of evolving cyber threats and robust safeguarding measures makes their voice not only credible but essential in today's increasingly digital landscape.

The author's professional journey is marked by a commitment to safeguarding organizations from cyber threats, having worked with a range of clients from local municipalities to central government departments across the UK. Their hands-on expertise has been instrumental in implementing and refining security protocols that address the contemporary challenges faced by enterprises. This diverse experience has solidified their reputation as a trusted resource in the cybersecurity field, establishing a strong foundation for sharing valuable insights through their writing.

Educated in advanced technologies and strategic communications, the author's academic background has shaped their approach to both cybersecurity and writing. Their desire to inform and educate about complex security issues stems from their own experiences in the military, where clarity and accessibility were paramount in training and operations. Writing this book emerged from a passion to demystify cybersecurity for a wider audience, showcasing that it is not just a concern for IT professionals but a universally relevant topic.

Blending a clear, engaging writing style with a passion for teaching, the author connects with audiences by making intricate topics accessible. They believe in the importance of practical knowledge and real-world examples in understanding the critical nature of cybersecurity. Personal anecdotes from their military career enrich their narrative, allowing readers to see the human side of cybersecurity beyond just policies and procedures.

Driven by a mission to empower organizations and individuals alike, the author is committed to fostering a culture of cybersecurity awareness. Their future goals include expanding their reach through workshops, consulting, and further publications, all with the aim of demystifying the complexities of cybersecurity. They envision a world where understanding cybersecurity is as fundamental as understanding technology itself, and are excited to contribute to this transformation.

Table of Contents

Chapter 1: Introduction to Cyber Security Supplier Assurance

Chapter 2: Understanding Supplier Risk Management

Chapter 3: Regulatory and Compliance Standards

Chapter 4: Supplier Due Diligence Processes

Chapter 5: Security Assessments and Testing Methodologies

Chapter 6: Code and Software Assurance

Chapter 7: Hardware Security Assessment

Chapter 8: Incident Response and Supplier Cooperation

(1) - 8.1 Developing Incident Response Plans with Suppliers

(2) - 8.2 Communication Protocols During Incidents

(3) - 8.3 Post-Incident Review Processes

Chapter 9: Building Effective Supplier Relationships

Chapter 10: Cyber Security Awareness Programs for Suppliers

Chapter 11: Leveraging Technology for Supplier Assurance

(1) - 11.1 Automation in Supplier Assessment Processes

(2) - 11.2 Utilizing Threat Intelligence Platforms

(3) - 11.3 Blockchain and its Role in Supply Chain Security

Chapter 12: Case Studies of Supplier Assurance Failures

Chapter 13: Future Trends in Supplier Cyber Security Assurance

Chapter 14: Developing a Supplier Assurance Framework

Chapter 15: Conclusion and Next Steps

(1) - 15.1 Key Takeaways from the Book

(2) - 15.2 Establishing Next Steps for Implementation

(3) - 15.3 The Importance of Ongoing Supplier Engagement

Chapter 1: Introduction to Cyber Security Supplier Assurance

1.1 Defining Cyber Security Supplier Assurance

Cyber Security Supplier Assurance is a critical concept aimed at safeguarding organizations from potential security risks associated with third-party vendors. In today's interconnected digital landscape, relying on suppliers for various services—from software to hardware—means that their security practices must align with your organization's standards. Supplier assurance involves a thorough evaluation of suppliers to ensure they have implemented adequate security measures. It includes assessing their policies, procedures, and compliance with industry regulations, ultimately ensuring that they are capable of protecting sensitive data. Without a robust supplier assurance process, organizations expose themselves to unforeseen vulnerabilities that could compromise their entire cyber ecosystem.

The relationship between supplier assurance and overall cybersecurity posture is integral to an organization's risk management strategy. Organizations must view their suppliers as extensions of their own cybersecurity infrastructure. A gap in a supplier's security could create a chink in the armor of an organization's defenses. Having a solid supplier assurance framework not only helps in identifying and managing risk but also enhances the organization's overall resilience against cyber threats. It fosters trust and facilitates smoother communication with suppliers, ensuring that they are on the same page regarding security expectations. An effective assurance strategy enhances overall cybersecurity posture by creating a more secure and reliable supply chain.

One practical approach to ensuring that suppliers meet assurance standards is through continuous monitoring and regular assessments. Engaging in periodic reviews of dependencies, validating compliance through audits, and requesting evidence of security practices are key elements in maintaining a secure supply chain. As cybersecurity threats evolve, it is vital to adapt supplier assurance practices to ensure they remain effective. This proactive stance not only protects sensitive data but also reinforces a culture of security within all levels of the organization, demonstrating a commitment to safeguarding resources against an ever-changing threat landscape.

1.2 Importance of Supplier Assurance in Cyber Security

Supplier assurance plays a critical role in preventing security breaches and securing networks. As organizations increasingly rely on external suppliers for various services and products, the risks associated with these partnerships grow significantly. Suppliers often have access to sensitive information and critical infrastructure, making their security practices a vital part of an organization's overall cybersecurity strategy. A lapse in a supplier's security can lead to vulnerabilities that criminals can exploit, thereby compromising entire systems. Therefore, assessing supplier security measures should not be viewed as an optional task but as an essential component of maintaining a secure operating environment.

Real-world incidents have consistently highlighted the importance of robust supplier security practices. For instance, the Target data breach in 2013 involved compromised credentials obtained from a third-party vendor, which led to the theft of millions of credit card details. This incident underscored how interconnected supply chains could become a pathway for cyber attacks. Similarly, the SolarWinds attack demonstrated that vulnerabilities in supplier software could have cascading effects across an entire industry. These examples serve as stark reminders that even well-established organizations can fall victim to cyber threats if their suppliers do not adhere to stringent security protocols. Cybersecurity professionals must thus ensure rigorous testing and validation of code, software, and hardware supplied by vendors before deployment to safeguard their own networks.

Effective supplier assurance requires an ongoing commitment to evaluate suppliers' security postures. This involves not only assessing their current practices but also establishing standards for continuous improvement. By integrating supplier security assessments into their risk management framework, organizations can ensure that they are not only compliant but are proactively addressing potential vulnerabilities. A practical step includes creating a detailed checklist of security controls that every supplier must meet before processing any sensitive data or systems. By demanding thorough security practices from suppliers and holding them accountable, cybersecurity professionals can significantly enhance their organization's defense against cyber threats.

1.3 Scope and Objectives of the Book

This book delves into critical themes and areas vital for cybersecurity professionals who engage with suppliers. It emphasizes the importance of establishing a robust assurance framework that encompasses the testing and validation of suppliers' code, software, and hardware before they are deployed into live environments. By focusing on risk management, compliance, and the principles of secure software development life cycles, professionals will gain insight into best practices that are essential for protecting their own networks and data. The discussions will also highlight the complexities of managing supply chain risks, advocating for transparent communication between businesses and their suppliers. This helps to build trust and ensures that all parties are aware of their responsibilities in maintaining cybersecurity standards.

The objectives of this book are clearly defined to guide cybersecurity professionals in their interactions with suppliers. It aims to illuminate the critical importance of rigorous testing and validation processes that suppliers must undergo to minimize vulnerabilities. Readers will learn how to assess supplier security practices effectively, ensuring that every piece of technology integrated into their systems adheres to a predefined set of standards. Furthermore, the book will encourage the adoption of a culture of continuous improvement in cybersecurity practices, pushing for regular audits and assessments. By equipping professionals with practical tools and frameworks, this book aims to enhance their ability to navigate the assurance landscape in the supply chain confidently.

Understanding the role of suppliers in your cybersecurity strategy is paramount. Regularly reviewing and updating assurance processes will create a more resilient cybersecurity posture. Implementing appropriate testing methods like penetration testing, code reviews, and vulnerability assessments will go a long way in fortifying organizational defenses against potential breaches.

Chapter 2: Understanding Supplier Risk Management

2.1 Types of Supplier Risks

Supplier risks, particularly from a cybersecurity standpoint, can encompass a variety of threats that organizations must navigate. These risks may arise from inadequate data protection practices, third-party access vulnerabilities, and the inherent flaws in the supply chain itself. For instance, a supplier may have poor security controls, making their systems a soft target for malware, which can compromise sensitive client data during transfer or storage. Additionally, a supplier's use of outdated software or hardware can introduce unforeseen vulnerabilities that could be exploited by malicious actors. This scenario underscores the importance of understanding the full ecosystem in which a supplier operates, including their network, the security of their own suppliers, and the robustness of the systems they use to deliver products or services.

Classifying these risks is crucial for effective management and mitigation because not all supplier risks are equal in severity or likelihood of occurrence. By developing a risk classification system, organizations can prioritize their efforts based on the potential impact on their operations and data integrity. Categorizing risks allows cybersecurity professionals to focus resources on the most significant threats while ensuring necessary precautions are established for lower-risk suppliers. This structured approach facilitates a more strategic communication pathway with suppliers, guiding them through specific security expectations and compliance requirements. Effective management hinges on this classification, allowing for actionable insights that support ongoing improvement and adaptation to the ever-evolving landscape of cyber threats. Understanding these nuances can empower organizations to establish a stronger assurance framework with their suppliers, mitigating risks before they become actual vulnerabilities.

Cybersecurity professionals must remain vigilant and proactive in their approach to supplier relationships. Regular risk assessments and continuous monitoring should be integrated into supplier management processes. Taking these steps not only protects the organization but also helps cultivate a culture of security throughout the supply chain. Organizations are advised to require suppliers to demonstrate assurance through rigorous testing and certification of their systems before integration. This not only resonates with cybersecurity best practices but also strengthens the trust relationship between organizations and their suppliers.

2.2 Risk Assessment Frameworks

Assessing supplier-related risks requires a systematic approach, and several established frameworks have emerged to guide organizations in this critical area. The NIST Cybersecurity Framework is widely recognized for its structured methodology that emphasizes the identification, protection, detection, response, and recovery processes relevant to suppliers. Similarly, the ISO 27001 standard provides a comprehensive framework for establishing, implementing, maintaining, and continually improving an information security management system (ISMS), which can include supplier relationships. Other notable frameworks include the FAIR (Factor Analysis of Information Risk) model, which quantifies risk in financial terms, helping organizations prioritize risk management decisions. Organizations often choose a combination of these frameworks to tailor their risk assessment strategies effectively, ensuring that their suppliers align with their security objectives and compliance requirements.

Selecting the right risk assessment framework is crucial and should align with the organization's specific needs and regulatory obligations. Organizations should start by evaluating their current risk profile, considering factors such as the types of suppliers they engage with, the nature of their data, and regulatory requirements they must adhere to. For instance, firms in highly regulated industries like finance or healthcare may need a more stringent approach, aligning with frameworks that emphasize compliance like ISO 27001 or NIST. Meanwhile, a growing software company may benefit from frameworks that promote Agile methodologies, allowing them to swiftly adapt and respond to emerging risks. Additionally, organizations should engage stakeholders from various domains—such as legal, compliance, and IT—to ensure that the selected framework addresses all pertinent aspects of their risk landscape.

As organizations navigate the complex web of supplier relationships, it is important to regularly reassess the chosen frameworks. Supplier environments can change rapidly, leading to new risks and vulnerabilities, making continuous improvement essential. Establishing a feedback loop where insights from risk assessments inform the framework's application will help organizations remain proactive while engaging suppliers. Consider conducting regular training sessions for stakeholders involved in supplier oversight to ensure everyone is updated on best practices and the latest developments in risk management frameworks. This ongoing commitment can significantly bolster an organization's resilience against supply chain threats.

2.3 Risk Mitigation Strategies

Minimizing supplier-related risks requires a thorough understanding of the dependencies inherent in modern supply chains, especially when it comes to cybersecurity. Engaging with suppliers means recognizing the potential threats they may pose, whether through data breaches, vulnerabilities in their software, or lapses in their security protocols. One effective strategy is to implement stringent vetting processes for all suppliers, involving security assessments that evaluate their cybersecurity posture. This includes reviewing their compliance with industry standards, such as ISO 27001 or NIST frameworks, and scrutinizing their past security incidents. Regular audits and reviews can also ensure suppliers maintain rigorous cybersecurity practices throughout the relationship. Establishing Service Level Agreements (SLAs) that include specific security obligations further reinforces accountability, creating a shared commitment to protecting sensitive data and systems.

Creating a proactive risk management culture within your organization is crucial for navigating the complexities of supplier relationships. This culture should prioritize open communication and collaboration regarding security practices among internal teams and external partners. Encouraging stakeholders to report potential risks without hesitation fosters an environment where concerns are addressed promptly. Training sessions and workshops on risk identification and mitigation strategies can equip employees with the necessary skills to recognize vulnerabilities in supplier interactions. Moreover, integrating continuous monitoring techniques, such as threat intelligence gathering and performance metrics evaluation, supports an agile response to any potential risks. This proactive stance not only enhances security but also builds trust with suppliers, demonstrating that your organization values security as a top priority.

Establishing clear procedures for incident response that involve suppliers is equally essential. An effective risk mitigation strategy incorporates joint crisis management plans, ensuring that both parties are prepared for potential breaches or disruptions. Documenting roles and responsibilities in the face of a security incident creates clarity and expedites response times. Regular drills and simulations can help both your organization and your suppliers stay ready for real-world situations, ultimately minimizing impact and fostering a resilient supply chain. Strengthening these relationships through transparency and shared goals in cybersecurity fosters a security-first mindset across all interactions, ultimately leading to a more secure and dependable supply network.

Chapter 3: Regulatory and Compliance Standards

3.1 Overview of Global Cyber Security Regulations

The landscape of global cyber security regulations is complex and constantly evolving, reflecting the dynamic nature of technology and threat environments. Various frameworks have emerged to guide organizations in establishing robust security protocols, particularly those that engage with suppliers across supply chains. Notable regulations such as the General Data Protection Regulation (GDPR) in the European Union, the Health Insurance Portability and Accountability Act (HIPAA) in the United States, and the Payment Card Industry Data Security Standard (PCI DSS) are crucial for shaping supplier security. GDPR emphasizes the protection of personal data, mandating organizations to ensure that suppliers comply with stringent privacy safeguards. HIPAA, on the other hand, focuses on the security of health information, requiring rigorous standards that suppliers must meet when handling sensitive health data. PCI DSS sets requirements for secure handling of credit card information, impacting how payment processors and related suppliers operate and interact with clients. These regulations not only aim to protect end users but also serve as a framework for organizations to assess the security posture of their suppliers.

The implications of these global regulations on supplier engagement practices are profound. Organizations must adopt a proactive approach in evaluating and ensuring compliance among their suppliers. This means instituting comprehensive due diligence processes that include in-depth assessments of a supplier's security policies, practices, and historical performance. Organizations need to regularly audit their suppliers' security controls and practices against regulatory requirements to mitigate any potential risks that could impact their own systems. Furthermore, integrating compliance checks into the supplier onboarding process ensures that new partnerships align with the organization's security and risk management strategies from the outset. The need for ongoing communication regarding compliance statuses and changes in regulations enhances trust and accountability in supplier relationships. This continuous interaction fosters a culture of transparency and shared responsibility for cybersecurity across the supply chain, helping organizations remain resilient in the face of emerging threats.

As organizations navigate these complex regulatory landscapes, a practical tip is to implement a supplier cybersecurity framework that aligns with key regulatory requirements. This framework should outline specific security measures and compliance obligations, helping to create clear expectations between the organization and its suppliers. Regular training sessions and workshops can also be beneficial in keeping all parties informed about the latest regulatory changes and best practices in cybersecurity. This ensures that both the organization and its suppliers are equipped with the knowledge and tools to effectively manage risks and enhance the overall security posture of their collaborative networks.

3.2 Understanding Compliance with Industry Standards

Adhering to industry-specific standards is vital for ensuring supplier compliance, particularly in fields where data integrity and security are paramount. Each sector may have distinct requirements that suppliers must meet. For example, in the healthcare industry, adherence to the Health Insurance Portability and Accountability Act (HIPAA) is essential for protecting patient information. In contrast, financial organizations might focus on the Payment Card Industry Data Security Standard (PCI DSS) to safeguard payment data. Understanding these standards allows cyber security professionals to identify the necessary certifications and mandates that suppliers must possess. This knowledge ensures that suppliers are equipped to manage sensitive data and maintain security protocols effectively, ultimately safeguarding the integrity of your own network and data.

To ensure that suppliers meet necessary compliance requirements, cyber security professionals must implement a structured assurance process. This involves assessing suppliers against defined criteria that align with relevant industry standards. Regular audits and risk assessments can facilitate this evaluation, providing insights into a supplier's compliance status and identifying potential vulnerabilities before they become critical issues. Establishing strong communication channels with suppliers is also essential. By fostering a transparent relationship, professionals can ensure that suppliers are aware of compliance expectations and can address any issues proactively. Documentation is another critical aspect; companies should require suppliers to provide detailed reports of compliance processes, which serve as tangible evidence of their adherence to industry standards.

Practically, developing a checklist based on industry standards can guide professionals in the compliance verification process. This checklist may include aspects such as reviewing third-party certifications, security policies, incident response plans, and past audit results. Engaging suppliers in regular training and updates related to compliance can also enhance their awareness and responsiveness to evolving standards. Ensuring that all code, software, and hardware undergo rigorous testing before deployment further adds a layer of assurance, helping to mitigate risks associated with non-compliance. By following these steps, cyber security professionals can fortify their networks against potential vulnerabilities introduced by third-party suppliers.

3.3 Frameworks for Supplier Compliance Audits

Frameworks for conducting compliance audits on suppliers are essential in ensuring that cybersecurity standards and best practices are upheld. These frameworks serve as structured guidelines that organizations can follow to assess the security posture of their suppliers, focusing on various aspects such as risk management, data protection, and regulatory adherence. The process typically involves defining the scope of the audit, identifying key performance indicators, and establishing assessment methodologies. Standards like ISO 27001, NIST SP 800-53, and COBIT are popular examples that can help inform an audit framework. Implementing a structured approach allows organizations to systematically evaluate their suppliers, ensuring that third parties are not only compliant but also aligned with the organization's overall cybersecurity objectives. Furthermore, a risk-based approach can help in prioritizing suppliers that pose higher risks, thus optimizing resources and enhancing the effectiveness of compliance efforts.

Best practices for maintaining compliance oversight across suppliers include regular communication, establishing clear compliance expectations, and conducting periodic assessments. It is crucial to foster a collaborative relationship with suppliers to ensure they understand the compliance requirements and the importance of adhering to them. Organizations should consider implementing continuous monitoring tools that provide real-time insights into supplier performance and compliance status. Utilizing technology can streamline the audit process, making it more efficient and less burdensome. Additionally, training and awareness programs for both internal teams and suppliers can build a robust culture of security and compliance. By incorporating feedback mechanisms and incident response plans, organizations can better manage compliance risks associated with suppliers. Documenting evidence of compliance activities not only aids in auditing but also promotes transparency and accountability across the supply chain.

The success of a supplier compliance audit framework often hinges on integrating these practices into the organization's overall cybersecurity strategy. A proactive approach not only helps in mitigating risks but also builds trust with suppliers, which is essential in cultivating long-term partnerships. It's advisable to review and refine the compliance framework regularly to adapt to changing regulations and emerging threats, ensuring that the organization remains resilient in a dynamic cyber landscape.

Chapter 4: Supplier Due Diligence Processes

4.1 Conducting Supplier Evaluations

Evaluating potential suppliers is a critical process that requires a systematic approach to ensure that they meet your organization's cybersecurity needs. The evaluation begins with identifying potential suppliers, followed by gathering relevant information about their services, products, and credibility. This involves reviewing their financial stability, market reputation, and any previous engagements with organizations similar to yours. You should also conduct interviews or meetings with key personnel from the supplier's organization to gauge their expertise and commitment to cybersecurity protocols. Once initial information is gathered, it's important to analyze and compare suppliers against your specific requirements and objectives. This includes examining their compliance with industry standards, certifications, and their historical performance regarding incident responses and breach handling.

Cybersecurity alignment is crucial when assessing suppliers. Establish specific criteria that vendors must meet to ensure that their standards and practices align with your organization's cybersecurity framework. These criteria should include the supplier's ability to conduct regular security assessments, implement robust access controls, and maintain a comprehensive incident response plan. It is also important to evaluate whether the suppliers adhere to data protection regulations and what measures they have in place to protect sensitive information. Their track record in patch management, vulnerability assessments, and penetration testing can provide insights into their proactive stance on cybersecurity. Integrating this information into your evaluation will help to mitigate risks associated with third-party engagements and ensure that all suppliers contribute positively to your cybersecurity posture.

During the evaluation process, make it a standard practice to request third-party audit reports and vulnerability assessments as part of your due diligence efforts. This will provide additional assurance regarding the supplier's security posture. Ensure that the evaluation does not end once the supplier is selected; establish a framework for ongoing monitoring and reassessment to stay ahead of any potential vulnerabilities as the cybersecurity landscape evolves. Understanding that supplier assessments should be a continuous process will help in maintaining robust security across your networks and data. As a final tip, consider collaborating with your suppliers when crafting security requirements and testing scenarios, as this can lead to a stronger partnership and a more secure supply chain.

4.2 Background Checks and Assessments

Background checks are a crucial step in the supplier selection process for organizations focused on cybersecurity. This is particularly important in a landscape where risks are growing, and supply chain vulnerabilities can lead to significant breaches. A thorough background check helps to verify the credibility of potential suppliers, ensuring they meet relevant legal, financial, and regulatory standards. By investigating a supplier's history, management practices, and any previous incidents of non-compliance or cyber breaches, organizations can significantly reduce the risk of partnering with unreliable entities. When cyber security professionals engage with suppliers, they must gather intelligence on past performances, client reviews, and compliance records. This sets a strong foundation for establishing trust and accountability, ultimately safeguarding critical networks and sensitive data.

Assessment methods play an essential role in evaluating supplier reliability beyond the initial background checks. Various strategies can be employed to assess their cybersecurity posture and overall ability to meet contractual obligations. One effective method is conducting comprehensive risk assessments, which can take several forms such as penetration testing, vulnerability assessments, and security audits. These assessments provide insights into a supplier's capabilities and can highlight potential weaknesses before they become critical issues. Furthermore, examining the supplier's adherence to industry standards and frameworks, such as ISO 27001 or the NIST Cybersecurity Framework, can offer additional reassurance about their commitment to cybersecurity best practices. Utilizing a combination of qualitative evaluations, performance metrics, and standardized benchmarks can create a more complete picture of a supplier's operational integrity.

When it comes to integrating suppliers into a broader supply chain, organizations must ensure that strict testing of code, software, and hardware takes place before any product or service goes live. Implementing a mandatory testing phase that includes security vulnerability scans and code reviews can be instrumental in identifying flaws and ensuring that only robust solutions are deployed. This not only elevates the security posture of the organization but also fosters a culture of accountability among suppliers. Regular communication and feedback loops between the organization and its suppliers can help maintain alignment on security goals. Cybersecurity professionals should be proactive, continuously seeking information on emerging threats and insisting on transparency from suppliers about their operations. By adopting these practices, organizations can help ensure that their partnerships with suppliers effectively bolster their cybersecurity frameworks.

4.3 Documentation and Record Keeping

Thorough documentation is a cornerstone of the supplier vetting process, particularly in the field of cybersecurity. When evaluating potential suppliers, it is crucial to keep detailed records of assessments, interactions, and evaluations. These documents serve as a comprehensive history of the decision-making process, reflecting transparency and due diligence. By meticulously documenting each step taken during the vetting process, cybersecurity professionals create a necessary audit trail that not only reinforces accountability but also provides essential insights into supplier capabilities and risks. This documentation protects organizations by ensuring that all decisions are backed by evidence, making it easier to demonstrate compliance with regulatory requirements and internal standards.

Maintaining accurate records of supplier assessments is equally vital. Best practices include creating standardized templates for evaluations to ensure consistency and clarity. Each supplier should be assessed against established criteria covering various aspects such as security protocols, compliance certifications, and past incidents. Regular updates should be integrated into the records to reflect any changes in the supplier's status or operations. Additionally, establishing a centralized digital repository for these documents enhances accessibility while safeguarding them with appropriate security measures. An organized approach not only simplifies retrieval and review processes but also fosters a culture of continuous improvement within the organization. By keeping well-documented records, cybersecurity professionals can easily revisit past evaluations, facilitating a more informed and efficient supplier management strategy.

One practical tip to enhance documentation practices is to implement a routine review schedule. Periodically assessing the completeness and relevance of documentation will help ensure that the information remains useful and up-to-date. This review should involve cross-referencing recorded information against the latest supplier communications and updates. By doing so, organizations can proactively manage risks associated with supplier relationships while ensuring a robust assurance route for their own networks and data.

Chapter 5: Security Assessments and Testing Methodologies

5.1 Types of Security Assessments

Security assessments are a crucial part of managing supplier security, particularly in today's environment where the interconnectivity of networks and data is paramount. Different types of security assessments are available, each tailored to uncover specific vulnerabilities and compliance issues that a supplier may present. Common types include vulnerability assessments, penetration testing, security audits, and risk assessments. A vulnerability assessment aims to identify weaknesses in a system, often through automated tools that scan for known vulnerabilities. Penetration testing is more hands-on, involving ethical hackers simulating an attack to see if they can exploit any vulnerabilities discovered. Security audits provide a comprehensive review of the security posture, looking at policies, processes, and controls in place. Risk assessments, on the other hand, evaluate potential risks and the impact they could have on the business, allowing organizations to make informed decisions about risk management and mitigation strategies.

The purpose of these assessments extends beyond simply identifying flaws. They serve as a critical checkpoint in the supplier evaluation process, ensuring that potential partners adhere to industry standards and best practices. By employing these assessments, Cyber Security Professionals gain insights that inform their decisions on supplier selection and ongoing management. Security assessments can uncover not only technical vulnerabilities but also operational weaknesses and gaps in compliance with regulatory frameworks. This identification process is vital, as a single oversight can lead to significant data breaches or supply chain disruptions. Furthermore, these assessments provide documented evidence of a supplier's commitment to security, helping organizations establish a robust security framework that aligns with their own practices and policies. As such, integrating a variety of security assessments into the procurement process can significantly bolster an organization's defenses and assure stakeholders of the supplier's reliability.

Choosing the right type of security assessment depends on various factors including the specific needs of the organization, the nature of the supplier relationship, and the regulatory environment in which the organization operates. Each type of assessment delivers unique insights and, when combined, offers a holistic view of the supplier's security posture. Regularly engaging in these assessments ensures that organizations can adapt to changing security landscapes and evolving threats. As a practical tip, organizations should develop a structured assessment schedule to ensure continual evaluation of supplier security, rather than relying solely on initial assessments. This ongoing approach can help catch potential issues early, protecting the organization from insight-heavy surprises down the line.

5.2 Penetration Testing Approaches

Penetration testing involves various methods that can be specifically tailored to assess the security of supplier systems. These methods include black box testing, where the tester has no prior knowledge of the system, and white box testing, where they have full access to the underlying architecture. Grey box testing combines elements of both approaches, simulating an attack from someone with limited knowledge of the system. By employing these different methodologies, security architects can gain a comprehensive understanding of potential vulnerabilities within supplier systems. Furthermore, it is essential to adjust the testing approach based on the specific context and technology stack of each supplier, ensuring a targeted and effective assessment.

Assessing vulnerabilities through simulated attacks is crucial for understanding the potential risks that could jeopardize network integrity and data security. By conducting penetration tests, organizations can identify weaknesses before malicious actors exploit them. This proactive approach allows for the implementation of necessary fixes and mitigation strategies well ahead of any real-world attacks. It also fosters a culture of security awareness among both suppliers and organizations, showcasing the importance of rigorous testing not only of code and software but also of hardware before it goes live. Ultimately, simulated attacks provide valuable insights into the overall security posture, enabling more informed decisions regarding supplier partnerships.

5.3 Continuous Monitoring and Validation

Ongoing monitoring of supplier security postures has become a critical requirement in today's threat landscape. As organizations increasingly rely on third-party suppliers, it is essential to continuously evaluate their security measures to ensure they are effectively safeguarding sensitive data and maintaining resilient infrastructures. Regular assessments help to identify vulnerabilities that may arise due to evolving threats, changes in business practices, or shifts in technology. These assessments should not be viewed as one-time events but rather as integral components of a holistic security strategy. Establishing a continuous monitoring framework enables organizations to keep pace with the dynamic nature of information security and ensures that suppliers adhere to the highest standards throughout the life cycle of their services or products.

Techniques for continuous validation of security measures can enhance the effectiveness of this monitoring process. Utilizing automated tools to conduct regular security assessments and tests can provide real-time insights into the security health of suppliers. These tools can help detect security weaknesses or policy non-compliance as soon as they emerge. Additionally, incorporating penetration testing within the validation process allows organizations to simulate real-world attack scenarios, offering a more thorough understanding of potential vulnerabilities. Developing strong communication channels with suppliers strengthens this continuous validation approach, enabling quick responses to identified issues and fostering a culture of transparency and accountability.

Regularly revisiting and updating security requirements in light of emerging threats and changes in the business environment is also advantageous. Leveraging frameworks such as the NIST Cybersecurity Framework or ISO 27001 can provide a solid foundation for ongoing evaluation and refinement of security protocols. Additionally, engaging in collaborative security exercises with suppliers can promote a shared understanding of threats and encourage proactive defense mechanisms. By adopting a mindset focused on continuous improvement in supplier security, organizations can protect their networks and data effectively, reducing the likelihood of breaches and maintaining the integrity of their supply chains.

Chapter 6: Code and Software Assurance

6.1 Secure Software Development Life Cycle (SDLC)

Building a secure software development life cycle (SDLC) is essential when engaging with suppliers. The principles of a secure SDLC should prioritize security at every stage of development, fostering a culture of security awareness and proactive risk management. Threat modeling and risk assessment must be integral parts of the initial planning phase, assessing potential vulnerabilities associated with the software components and the infrastructure in which they will function. Ensuring that security requirements are clearly defined can enhance collaboration between suppliers and your organization. Security training for development teams should be ongoing, with an emphasis on secure coding practices to mitigate common vulnerabilities. This can help in tailoring secure development processes that align with both your organization's standards and the supplier's capabilities.

The incorporation of security measures must span all key phases of the software development life cycle, starting from the requirements gathering to deployment. During the requirements phase, security must be defined as a primary functional requirement. As the design progresses, architects should include security best practices that allow for robust solutions while remaining adaptive to changes. In development, security testing should not just be an afterthought; this includes static and dynamic analysis to identify possible weaknesses in the code. During the testing phase, comprehensive penetration testing should simulate real-world attacks to evaluate security postures and compliance. Finally, the deployment phase requires careful adherence to security protocols to safeguard against operational risks. Continuous monitoring and updating in response to emerging threats is crucial after the software goes live, ensuring that security remains an ongoing commitment rather than a final checkpoint in the development process. Regular audits of the supplier's security practices can help ensure compliance and risk mitigation over time.

Cybersecurity professionals must ensure that there is a strong contractual agreement in place that mandates compliance with these secure SDLC principles. These contracts should include clauses requiring suppliers to follow specific security standards, conduct regular security assessments, and ensure that all personnel involved in the development process are adequately trained. By setting clear expectations and fostering collaboration, organizations can better protect their networks and data. Implementing a secure SDLC not only enhances the quality of software but also significantly contributes to reducing potential security risks associated with third-party integrations.

6.2 Code Review Practices and Tools

Conducting thorough code reviews is a critical step in identifying vulnerabilities within software. Best practices emphasize the importance of establishing a systematic approach to code reviews. It is essential to create clear guidelines that define the objectives and scope of each review, allowing reviewers to focus on specific areas such as security flaws, performance issues, and adherence to coding standards. Engaging multiple reviewers in a collaborative environment can enhance the review process, as diverse perspectives often uncover different vulnerabilities. Effective communication among team members is vital, enabling them to provide constructive feedback and ask pertinent questions related to the code in question. Ensuring that all changes are documented can facilitate future reviews and enable a better understanding of the software's evolution over time. Adopt a mindset of continuous improvement, where lessons learned from past reviews lead to refining the review process itself, making it more efficient and comprehensive with each iteration.

Utilizing the right tools can significantly enhance the effectiveness of the code review process, especially when dealing with complex supplier codebases. Automated code analysis tools can be leveraged to identify common vulnerabilities and security flaws quickly, serving as a first line of defense before manual review. Tools such as SonarQube and Fortify Static Code Analyzer not only highlight issues but also provide recommendations for remediation, streamlining the review process. Integrating collaborative platforms like GitHub or GitLab facilitates peer reviews, as they allow for efficient code sharing and commenting directly on changes. These platforms often include features like pull requests and built-in code review workflows that encourage active participation and ensure that all changes undergo scrutiny before merging. When evaluating supplier codebases, it is beneficial to prioritize tools that offer seamless integration with your existing development and testing environments, ensuring that security is baked into the software development lifecycle. This proactive approach to code review not only mitigates risks but also fosters a culture of quality and accountability.

Being proactive in code reviews leads to discovering vulnerabilities early in the software development lifecycle, which is crucial for maintaining the security and reliability of your systems. Consider formal training sessions for team members on identifying specific types of vulnerabilities like SQL injection or cross-site scripting. This not only strengthens their skills but also enriches the collective knowledge of the team. Pairing junior developers with experienced reviewers can also help cultivate a deeper understanding of secure coding practices. Emphasize the importance of following up on findings from code reviews—not just the fixes, but also confirming that the addressed vulnerabilities do not reappear in future iterations. Incorporating a feedback loop whereby suggestions from previous reviews influence current practices can lead to an ongoing enhancement of coding standards. Establishing a sprint or regular checkpoint dedicated solely to code review can create a disciplined schedule that reinforces these practices throughout the development life cycle.

6.3 Vulnerability Management in Software

Effective vulnerability management in supplier-developed software hinges on proactive strategies that focus on identifying, assessing, and mitigating security flaws before they can be exploited. Cyber Security Professionals must work closely with suppliers to ensure that appropriate processes are in place for vulnerability detection. Regular security assessments, including penetration testing and automated scanning tools, are essential in this regard. It's also vital to establish clear communication channels with suppliers, ensuring that any discovered vulnerabilities are reported and addressed promptly. This collaboration fosters an environment where security best practices become a shared priority and encourages the adoption of secure coding guidelines across development teams.

Timely remediation is critical in the vulnerability management process. After identifying a vulnerability, it should be prioritized based on its severity and potential impact on the organization. Cyber Security Architects need to engage in continuous dialogue with their internal teams and those of suppliers, establishing a streamlined process for fixing vulnerabilities. This cooperation not only accelerates remediation timelines but also helps to build trust and transparency with suppliers. Implementing a robust vulnerability lifecycle management program will help organizations track the status of identified vulnerabilities and ensure that appropriate actions are taken to remediate them efficiently.

The importance of rigorous testing cannot be overstated when it comes to deploying supplier-developed software. Cyber Security Professionals must advocate for thorough testing of software code, applications, and underlying hardware before integration into production environments. Employing a combination of static and dynamic analysis tools can aid in uncovering potential issues early in the development cycle. Furthermore, creating a culture of security within supplier organizations through training and awareness initiatives can lead to improved software quality and reduced risk. As security threats continuously evolve, fostering an environment that emphasizes ongoing testing and evaluation will ensure that vulnerabilities are managed effectively, allowing organizations to maintain the integrity of their networks and data.

Chapter 7: Hardware Security Assessment

7.1 Evaluating Hardware Security Measures

To effectively assess the hardware security of suppliers, it is critical to establish clear evaluation criteria that encompass various dimensions of hardware integrity and performance. Key aspects to focus on include the vendor's history of security incidents, their compliance with industry regulations, and the certifications they hold related to hardware security. A thorough understanding of how suppliers manage their supply chain is also vital, as vulnerabilities can be introduced at any stage of hardware production and distribution. It is important for cybersecurity architects to ask pointed questions regarding the supplier's practices for identifying and mitigating risks, such as how they validate the authenticity of their components and what measures they have in place for addressing potential hardware tampering. Evaluating suppliers on their commitment to continuous improvement in security practices can help ensure that they maintain a proactive approach towards emerging threats.

In addition to established evaluation criteria, the significance of robust physical security practices cannot be overstated. Physical security measures are essential to safeguard hardware from unauthorized access or tampering. This may include secure facilities, surveillance systems, and stringent access controls that limit who can interact with sensitive hardware components. It is crucial to recognize that even the most advanced cybersecurity protocols can be rendered ineffective if the physical devices themselves are not adequately protected. Cybersecurity professionals must assess the physical security measures of suppliers as part of their overall evaluation, ensuring suppliers maintain a secure environment for hardware development and deployment. Effective physical safeguards not only protect the hardware from direct threats but also reinforce the integrity of the broader supply chain, assuring that components are delivered free from potential breaches.

Ensuring that suppliers adhere to rigorous hardware testing methodologies before devices go live is a critical step in maintaining a secure architecture. Engaging in collaborative testing processes, such as penetration testing or vulnerability assessments, can provide valuable insights into the resilience of the hardware against various attack vectors. Cybersecurity professionals should advocate for transparent reporting of test results as well as any remediations performed following security assessments. This collaborative approach not only enhances the relationship with suppliers but also aids in building a more robust cybersecurity posture for the entire supply chain.

7.2 Supply Chain Integrity for Hardware Components

Supply chain integrity is crucial for ensuring hardware security. With an increasing reliance on technology across various sectors, the authenticity and reliability of hardware components can no longer be taken for granted. Compromised hardware can introduce vulnerabilities that jeopardize entire networks and sensitive data, making supply chain integrity a non-negotiable priority for cyber security professionals. The integrity of the supply chain encompasses all stages of hardware production, from the sourcing of raw materials and the manufacturing processes to distribution and installation. Any lapses at any of these stages can result in the insertion of malicious components or the use of counterfeit products, which can severely compromise the security posture of organizations.

To ensure the authenticity and reliability of hardware components, several methods can be employed. First, implementing strict supplier vetting processes is essential. Organizations should conduct thorough background checks on suppliers to evaluate their reputations and practices. Certifications, such as ISO standards, can serve as indicators of a supplier's commitment to quality and security. Furthermore, regular audits and assessments of supplier facilities can help verify that the manufacturing processes meet the required security protocols. Utilizing blockchain technology for tracking and verifying the entire journey of hardware from the manufacturer to the end-user is an emerging solution that offers transparency and traceability. In addition to these measures, engaging in secure design principles during the hardware development phase helps in identifying potential vulnerabilities early in the lifecycle. Such proactive measures ensure that products meet both the functional and security requirements before they reach the market.

Maintaining supply chain integrity requires ongoing vigilance. Developing strong partnerships with suppliers, coupled with clear communication about expectations concerning security standards, plays a vital role in fostering shared responsibility. Organizations should also stay informed about threat intelligence related to hardware vulnerabilities, which will assist in identifying potential risks and responding proactively. Rigorous testing of hardware components through simulated attacks can further ascertain their resilience against exploitation. Embracing a culture of security that involves continuous improvement in supply chain practices can significantly enhance the overall security posture of an organization. For those in the cyber security realm, establishing a comprehensive assessment framework to evaluate the security of hardware components sourced from suppliers can be a decisive step towards building a more secure infrastructure.

7.3 Security Testing for IoT Devices

The rise of Internet of Things (IoT) devices has opened new avenues for innovation, efficiency, and connectivity. However, these devices also introduce specific security challenges that cybersecurity professionals must address, particularly those stemming from product suppliers. One significant issue is the variability in security standards among manufacturers. Different suppliers often have different approaches to security, resulting in devices that may have weak points, outdated protocols, or insufficient patching practices. This variation can lead to vulnerabilities that put entire networks at risk, allowing adversaries to exploit unsecured devices and gain entry into otherwise secure environments. Additionally, many IoT devices operate with minimal computing power and resources, forcing manufacturers to prioritize functionality over robust security measures. These challenges highlight the urgency for cybersecurity professionals to engage with suppliers proactively, demanding transparency in their security practices and assurance that rigorous testing has been conducted before deployment.

Effective security testing methodologies for IoT hardware are essential to ensuring device integrity and safeguarding critical data. Traditional testing methods may not suffice due to the unique characteristics of IoT devices, which often include limited user interfaces and direct internet connectivity. Therefore, professionals must adopt a set of tailored strategies designed specifically for IoT contexts. One key methodology involves threat modeling, which identifies potential vulnerabilities and areas of exploitation based on device functionality and deployment scenarios. This is followed by penetration testing that mimics real-world attacks to assess the robustness of device defenses. Furthermore, continuous monitoring and vulnerability assessments post-deployment are crucial. As IoT devices often receive firmware updates, ongoing security evaluations help maintain a security posture capable of adapting to new threats. Utilizing automated testing tools can significantly aid these efforts, allowing for regular assessments without excessive manual intervention, thus ensuring that security protocols continually align with evolving risks.

As a practical tip, cybersecurity professionals should advocate for a zero-trust approach when working with IoT devices. This means assuming that potential threats exist within and outside the network and verifying every connection and transaction. By focusing on strong authentication measures, encrypting data both at rest and in transit, and regularly auditing supplier security practices, organizations can build a resilient defense against the specific challenges presented by IoT vendors. Furthermore, establishing clear communication channels with suppliers regarding security expectations can foster a culture of accountability, ensuring that both parties prioritize rigorous security testing alongside innovation.

Chapter 8: Incident Response and Supplier Cooperation

8.1 Developing Incident Response Plans with Suppliers

Collaboration with suppliers in developing incident response plans is crucial for ensuring the integrity of security protocols. The interconnectedness of supply chains means that a breach in one partner can compromise the entire network. By engaging suppliers in the planning process, organizations can align their incident response strategies, ensuring that everyone understands their roles and responsibilities during a crisis. Establishing clear communication channels before an incident occurs enables swift action and minimizes the impact of potential breaches. This collaboration fosters trust and enhances preparedness, transforming incident response from a solitary effort into a unified front.

Creating effective incident response plans involves a structured framework that encourages thorough analysis and continuous improvement. Begin by assessing risks associated with each supplier and identifying critical assets that could be affected by potential incidents. Establish defined roles for each party involved, detailing who will handle notifications, investigations, and follow-up actions. Regularly conduct joint exercises to test the effectiveness of the incident response plan, adapting it as necessary based on findings and evolving threats. This iterative process helps ensure that the response plan remains relevant and effective, safeguarding the organization's data, operations, and reputation.

It is vital to focus on ensuring that all suppliers undergo rigorous testing of their code, software, and hardware before integrating them into the production environment. Developing a checklist that includes security assessments, vulnerability scans, and compliance checks can help in standardizing this practice. Encourage suppliers to share their testing methodologies and results, which can lead to improved security posture for both parties. Building a culture of accountability and continuous improvement within the supply chain will not only strengthen individual supplier relationships but also ensure that the wider ecosystem remains resilient against cyber threats.

8.2 Communication Protocols During Incidents

Effective communication strategies play a pivotal role in enhancing collaboration during security incidents. When an incident occurs, the ability to quickly and efficiently share information among team members and stakeholders can significantly influence the outcome. Establishing a structured communication plan ensures that all parties are aware of their roles, responsibilities, and the current status of the incident. It's essential to utilize clear and precise language to prevent misunderstandings that may arise from ambiguous terminology. Using standardized terminologies, such as the Incident Command System, helps streamline communication across diverse teams, whether they are internal or external, and can facilitate consensus on priority actions. Consistent updates are critical; therefore, appointing a communication lead to disseminate timely information can keep all relevant parties aligned and responsive.

The importance of timely and transparent communication during an incident cannot be overstated. Delays in informing stakeholders can exacerbate the situation, leading to confusion and potentially allowing vulnerabilities to be exploited further. Transparency not only fosters trust but also allows for better decision-making among teams. By providing regular updates about what is known, what actions are being taken, and what support is needed, organizations can keep everyone involved and engaged throughout the incident lifecycle. This openness encourages a culture of collaboration, where all team members feel empowered to contribute their expertise and insights. Establishing a feedback loop enhances this process, allowing for continual adjustments and improvements in communication practices. In sensitive scenarios, where communication with suppliers is involved, it is crucial to manage public messaging thoughtfully to uphold reputation while maintaining operational security.

As part of these protocols, it is also beneficial to conduct post-incident reviews focusing on communication effectiveness. This analysis helps identify any gaps or weaknesses in protocols that may need to be addressed for future incidents. Incorporating lessons learned into the communication strategy ensures readiness for upcoming challenges. Cybersecurity professionals should emphasize the necessity of clear communication with suppliers to ensure they uphold the same standards of assurance, particularly when their products or services directly impact the organization's security posture. Regular training sessions on incident communication can also bolster preparedness, making sure that when an incident does occur, the response is not only swift but also coordinated and effective. Remember, it's essential to equip your teams with communication tools and training prior to an incident, as a proactive approach is often the best defense against the chaos of unexpected crises.

8.3 Post-Incident Review Processes

Conducting thorough post-incident reviews with suppliers is essential in today's complex cyber landscape. When a security incident occurs, it is imperative to collaborate closely with suppliers to systematically understand the causes and impacts of the event. This collaboration fosters transparency and accountability, allowing both parties to pinpoint vulnerabilities in the supplier's systems or processes that may have contributed to the incident. Engaging in these reviews not only helps to mitigate immediate risks but also builds a resilient relationship with suppliers, reinforcing the commitment to uphold high security standards. By addressing gaps discovered during the incident, organizations can enhance their security posture and develop strategies that ensure supplier compliance with their security protocols.

Extracting lessons learned is a critical element of shaping future security practices. By analyzing what went wrong, identifying effective responses, and scrutinizing the decision-making processes during the incident, cybersecurity professionals can compile valuable insights. This information can be instrumental in refining existing security frameworks and implementing robust testing protocols for code, software, and hardware. Creating a culture that prioritizes continuous improvement ensures that past incidents do not simply become historical footnotes but evolve into catalysts for strengthening defenses and enhancing operational resilience. Likewise, developing a comprehensive documentation process for each incident enables teams to track progress over time and establish benchmarks for measuring improvement.

Prioritizing these reviews and lessons learned promotes a proactive rather than reactive approach to cybersecurity. Establishing clear procedures for incident documentation, evaluation, and follow-up can greatly improve accountability, not only within your organization but also throughout the supply chain. By consistently applying what is learned from past experiences, organizations can increase their confidence in their suppliers' ability to secure networks and data, ultimately creating a safer digital environment for all stakeholders. Regular, structured post-incident reviews not only safeguard against future threats but also encourage a deeper partnership with suppliers, vital for cultivating trust in an increasingly interconnected world.

Chapter 9: Building Effective Supplier Relationships

9.1 Supplier Engagement Strategies

Effectively engaging with suppliers in cybersecurity matters begins with a clear understanding of expectations and requirements. Cybersecurity architects must articulate specific security protocols and standards that all suppliers must adhere to. This includes comprehensive guidelines regarding data protection, incident response, and risk management. Establishing a formalized framework for these expectations ensures that suppliers are not only aware of what is required but also understand the rationale behind these security measures. Regular engagement in dialogue can help build trust and transparency, as it allows both parties to discuss potential vulnerabilities and improvements, ensuring everyone is aligned with the overarching security objectives.

Fostering strong communication and collaboration with suppliers is crucial for building lasting partnerships in the cybersecurity realm. Establishing open lines of communication encourages suppliers to voice their concerns and suggestions, which can lead to enhanced security practices. Regular meetings, feedback sessions, and collaborative projects can help reinforce this relationship. Additionally, sharing insights on emerging threats and vulnerabilities within the industry can enhance the overall security posture of both the organization and its suppliers. When cyber security professionals and suppliers work closely together, it creates a sense of shared accountability, which is vital for anticipating and responding to cybersecurity incidents efficiently. This collaborative approach not only fortifies the supplier relationship but also significantly contributes to a more robust defense against cyber threats.

As an actionable tip, consider implementing a supplier security assessment program that includes regular audits and performance reviews. This not only ensures that suppliers are consistently meeting cybersecurity standards but also provides an opportunity for ongoing education and improvement of both parties' security measures.

9.2 Joint Risk Management Initiatives

Promoting joint risk management efforts between organizations and suppliers is essential in today's interconnected digital landscape. The complexities of supply chain dynamics require a collaborative approach, where both parties engage in transparent discussions about potential risks. This means establishing clear channels of communication that allow for the sharing of risk data, incident reports, and mitigation strategies. By working closely together, organizations and their suppliers can identify vulnerabilities early on and adopt preemptive measures. This partnership not only allows for a more comprehensive view of risk exposure but also reinforces trust between parties, fostering an environment where both can focus on innovation and growth while staying ahead of potential threats.

The benefits of a unified approach to managing risks are substantial. When organizations align their risk management frameworks with those of their suppliers, they create a cohesive strategy that enhances overall security posture. This strategical alignment minimizes the potential for gaps in defenses that attackers might exploit. Furthermore, shared risk understanding enables more effective prioritization of resources, ensuring that attention is directed towards the highest risks. A collaborative framework also simplifies compliance with regulatory requirements, as both parties can work together to uphold standards and demonstrate a commitment to security. Ultimately, organizations that adopt a unified approach achieve greater resilience, shortening response times during incidents, and improving their ability to recover from disruptions.

Continuous dialogue and regular joint assessments are vital to the success of joint risk management initiatives. Cyber security professionals should engage suppliers in ongoing discussions about security practices, evolving threats, and innovative solutions. This proactive engagement ensures that both organizations remain agile and responsive to the ever-changing threat landscape. One practical tip is to establish a routine schedule for joint risk assessments and penetration tests, where both the organization and suppliers participate. This not only enhances security measures but also deepens the collaborative relationship, creating a shared responsibility for cybersecurity across the supply chain.

9.3 Performance Metrics and Reviews

Establishing effective performance metrics is vital for assessing the security postures of suppliers. Organizations must clearly define what constitutes acceptable security practices, quantitatively measuring parameters such as compliance with security frameworks, incident response times, and the outcomes of regular vulnerability assessments. Metrics should also evaluate training completion rates among supplier employees, ensuring they are adequately prepared to face cyber threats. Additional elements to consider include the frequency of security updates, patch management efficacy, and third-party assessment results. When assessing these metrics, it is crucial to track long-term trends rather than one-off spikes, which can provide a clearer picture of a supplier's overall security reliability and maturity.

The review process is equally important in evaluating supplier performance and ensuring ongoing alignment with security expectations. Regularly scheduled reviews should be implemented, ideally on a quarterly or bi-annual basis, to discuss performance against the established metrics. During these reviews, it is essential to foster open communication, where both parties can discuss successes and areas for improvement. Tools such as scorecards can help visualize performance trends and areas that require immediate attention. An effective review process also includes action items with specific timelines for addressing identified weaknesses, ensuring that suppliers remain accountable. Continuous improvement should be the goal, while also integrating lessons learned from previous engagements to enhance future supplier relationships.

Ultimately, a robust framework built around these performance metrics and review processes not only instills confidence but also cultivates a culture of security that benefits both the supplier and the organization. As a practical tip, consider creating a checklist that focuses on key metrics and review questions that can be easily referenced during supplier assessments and discussions. This checklist can help practitioners remain thorough and consistent in their evaluations, ensuring that no critical aspects of security performance are overlooked.

Chapter 10: Cyber Security Awareness Programs for Suppliers

10.1 Training and Awareness Foundations

Training on cybersecurity for suppliers is crucial, as it serves as the bedrock upon which secure partnerships are established. Suppliers interact with various networks, platforms, and data that are integral to the operations of any organization. They are often considered the first line of defense against threats, which is why their understanding of security practices is essential. A comprehensive training program ensures that suppliers are aware of the specific requirements and standards expected of them, including compliance with regulations and industry best practices. Such training not only covers the technical aspects of cybersecurity but also emphasizes the significance of creating a culture of security that permeates their operations. Properly trained suppliers are more likely to recognize potential vulnerabilities and to respond effectively to incidents, which helps to mitigate risk across the entire supply chain.

Awareness is not just an add-on; it is a fundamental component that helps to reduce human errors that can lead to security breaches. Even the most sophisticated technology cannot fully safeguard against the mistakes made by individuals who are unaware of the risks involved. By fostering a heightened sense of awareness among employees and suppliers alike, organizations can significantly decrease the likelihood of security lapses. Awareness campaigns, alongside regular training sessions, can strengthen the understanding of common threats such as phishing attacks, malware, and social engineering tactics. By making security an ongoing conversation and integrating it into daily routines, everyone involved becomes a more vigilant participant in the defense against cyber threats. Each member, aware of their role and the potential consequences of their actions, can contribute to a more robust security posture for the entire organization.

Providing ongoing training and promoting awareness should not be seen as a one-time effort but rather as an evolving practice that adapts to new developments in the cybersecurity landscape. Regular updates to training materials and awareness programs can help keep suppliers informed about the latest threats, ensuring that they remain vigilant and well-prepared to tackle the challenges of an increasingly complex cyber environment. Building these foundations of training and awareness establishes trust and reinforces the idea that securing networks and data is a shared responsibility, extending beyond the boundaries of a single organization.

10.2 Tailoring Programs for Diverse Suppliers

Customizing awareness programs for various supplier types is not just beneficial; it is essential for a robust cybersecurity posture. Different suppliers bring unique challenges and risks depending on their size, industry, and technical capabilities. For instance, a large cloud service provider may have vastly different security practices and compliance requirements compared to a small software vendor or a hardware manufacturer. Recognizing these distinctions allows cybersecurity professionals to tailor training content that target suppliers' specific needs and contexts. By incorporating industry-relevant scenarios and examples, organizations can ensure that suppliers understand not only the importance of cybersecurity but also how it directly affects their products and the systems they integrate with. This relatability greatly increases engagement, making it easier for suppliers to grasp complex concepts and apply them in practical settings.

When designing effective training initiatives for these diverse suppliers, best practices must be employed to maximize impact. First, assessing the baseline cybersecurity knowledge of suppliers is crucial. This assessment allows organizations to identify gaps and tailor content accordingly. Interactive elements, such as simulations and hands-on exercises, can encourage participation and create a memorable learning experience. Furthermore, engaging different learning styles through a mix of visual, auditory, and kinesthetic materials ensures that training resonates with all participants. Regular updates to the content, based on emerging threats and industry changes, keep training relevant and valuable. Additionally, fostering a culture of open communication encourages suppliers to ask questions and seek clarity, thus promoting a more profound understanding of their responsibilities in the cybersecurity chain. A practical tip for implementation is to schedule follow-up sessions post-training to review key concepts and reinforce learning. This approach not only sustains interest but also solidifies the knowledge imparted during initial training sessions.

10.3 Evaluating Training Effectiveness

Assessing the effectiveness of supplier cybersecurity training is crucial to ensuring that third-party providers are adequately prepared to defend against potential threats. One effective method is to employ a combination of pre and post-training assessments. Before the training begins, participants can take a baseline test that evaluates their current cybersecurity knowledge and awareness. Following the training session, a similar assessment can be administered to measure knowledge retention and behavioral changes. This allows organizations to quantify improvements and establish whether the training met its objectives. Additionally, simulated phishing attacks can be utilized to determine how well the suppliers apply what they have learned in a real-world context. By measuring response rates to these simulated threats before and after training, organizations can gauge not only the immediate impact of the training but also its effectiveness over time.

Beyond assessment, establishing a feedback loop is essential for the continuous improvement of training programs. Encouraging suppliers to provide feedback on the training sessions fosters an atmosphere of collaboration and reflection. This input can guide modifications to the curriculum, ensuring it addresses the most pressing threats and aligns with the evolving cybersecurity landscape. Furthermore, organizations should regularly review incident reports and performance metrics to identify knowledge gaps or common areas of failure post-training. Integrating this information into the training process allows for a responsive training framework that adapts to new challenges. Continuous evaluation and adjustment not only enhance the skillset of suppliers but also strengthen the overall supply chain resilience against cyber threats, ensuring their defenses remain robust and up-to-date.

Incorporating routine evaluations not only helps maintain high training standards but also builds accountability among suppliers. By establishing clear benchmarks and performance indicators, organizations can better assure themselves that their suppliers are consistently meeting expected cybersecurity practices. Continuous improvement works best when it is coupled with transparent communication. Regular check-ins can motivate suppliers to be proactive about their cybersecurity stance while facilitating a culture where everyone invests in enhancing security measures. As the cyber threat landscape is always evolving, staying ahead of potential risks through ongoing training and assessment becomes a shared responsibility that ultimately protects both the organization and its suppliers.

Chapter 11: Leveraging Technology for Supplier Assurance

11.1 Automation in Supplier Assessment Processes

Automation can significantly streamline the supplier assessment process by eliminating cumbersome manual tasks that often lead to delays and inconsistencies. By integrating automated tools, organizations can ensure that the evaluation of suppliers is conducted systematically, allowing for faster and more reliable decision-making. This process involves the standardization of data collection, risk assessments, compliance checks, and performance evaluations. Automation allows for the seamless gathering of essential supplier information across multiple platforms, creating a centralized repository that is easily accessible and regularly updated. Furthermore, automated systems can reduce human error and enhance transparency, providing cyber security architects with a clear view of supplier capabilities and weaknesses.

Several specialized tools are available that enhance efficiency in the supplier assessment process. For instance, supplier risk management software can track compliance with security standards and provide real-time alerts for any deviations. Such tools can facilitate automated questionnaires that suppliers can complete, ensuring consistent data collection and reducing the administrative burden on assessment teams. Additionally, data analytics platforms can help cyber security professionals analyze trends in supplier performance, allowing them to make well-informed decisions and prioritize their assessments based on risk levels. By employing these advanced tools, organizations can ensure a thorough vetting process, enabling them to select suppliers that meet stringent security requirements before any engagements take place. Ensuring that these evaluations are rigorously conducted not only helps protect an organization's own network and data but also fortifies the entire supply chain against potential vulnerabilities.

As a practical tip, cyber security professionals should regularly review and update the criteria used for supplier assessments to keep pace with the ever-evolving cyber threat landscape. This proactive approach to refining your assessment processes can enhance the overall resilience and security posture of your organization while establishing a robust framework for supplier assurance.

11.2 Utilizing Threat Intelligence Platforms

Threat intelligence plays a pivotal role in enhancing supplier security assessments. By aggregating and analyzing data on emerging threats, organizations can gain critical insights into potential vulnerabilities that may affect their suppliers. This data-driven approach aids in identifying which third-party vendors may pose a risk to the overall security posture of the organization. The intelligence gathered can reveal patterns of exploitation, attack trends, and even specific vulnerabilities that may reside within a supplier's infrastructure. Armed with this information, security teams can carry out more informed assessments, prioritizing their evaluation efforts based on the threat profiles associated with different suppliers, thus allowing for a more strategic allocation of resources.

Integrating threat intelligence into supplier monitoring protocols enhances real-time oversight and vigilance. By embedding threat intelligence feeds into monitoring systems, organizations can continuously track supplier activities and any indicators of compromise. These feeds provide timely information on potential threats from outside, as well as notifications about unusual behavior within a supplier's environment. This integration ensures that any deviations from normal operations are promptly addressed, enabling organizations to promptly react to changes that could indicate a risk to their data and infrastructure. As suppliers increasingly become points of vulnerability due to third-party risks, proactive monitoring becomes an essential component of security assurance. It not only reassures organizations that their suppliers adhere to security best practices but also creates a culture of accountability among suppliers, fostering a more secure ecosystem overall.

To make the most of threat intelligence platforms, organizations should prioritize establishing clear collaboration channels with suppliers. This partnership ensures that all parties share relevant intelligence that can enhance mutual security. By engaging suppliers in active discussions about threat intelligence findings, organizations can help them understand their own exposure and improve their security measures in alignment with industry standards. Additionally, investing in training for both internal teams and suppliers on the use of threat intelligence platforms can yield significant returns. It builds capacity to act on insights provided, ensuring rigorous testing of code, software, and hardware before deployment. Ultimately, effective utilization of threat intelligence platforms can transform supplier relationships, turning them from potential liabilities into partners in resilience.

11.3 Blockchain and its Role in Supply Chain Security

Blockchain technology significantly enhances transparency and security within supply chains by providing a decentralized ledger that records transactions in an immutable and transparent manner. This capability builds trust among stakeholders, as every participant in the supply chain can access real-time data about the status and history of goods without the risk of tampering. Each transaction is securely linked to the previous one, making it easy to trace the movement of products from the origin to the final destination. This level of traceability not only helps in verifying the authenticity of products but also serves as a formidable barrier against fraud and unauthorized modifications. By ensuring that all parties have access to the same information, blockchain eliminates discrepancies and fosters greater collaboration among suppliers, manufacturers, and retailers. This transparency can be especially valuable in industries where compliance with regulations and standards is crucial, allowing companies to demonstrate due diligence and uphold ethical practices.

Practical applications of blockchain can be seen in various initiatives aimed at verifying supplier integrity. For instance, organizations can implement blockchain-based systems to assess and monitor the compliance of suppliers against pre-established criteria. Each supplier can be assigned a unique digital identity, allowing their credentials to be securely stored and accessed. When a supplier submits documentation—be it certifications, compliance reports, or quality assurances—these records can be permanently recorded on the blockchain, preventing alterations or duplicity. Additionally, smart contracts can be integrated into the supply chain process to automate various functions, such as releasing payments only upon verification of the delivery and quality of goods. This ensures that payments are securely tied to the actual performance of suppliers, motivating them to maintain high standards and further fostering a culture of accountability. Furthermore, real-time data sharing via the blockchain can help cybersecurity professionals identify potential weak points in their supply chains, enabling proactive measures to secure their networks and data against emerging threats.

As cybersecurity professionals engage with suppliers, emphasizing the importance of sharing accurate blockchain-based information can be a powerful tool for ensuring adherence to security protocols. It is essential for organizations to not only require suppliers to comply with cybersecurity standards but also to establish mechanisms for continual verification through blockchain. By leveraging this technology, companies can create a robust ecosystem that not only secures their supply routes but also builds a culture of trust and minimizing risk across all interactions. Embracing blockchain as a tool for supplier assurance can lead to innovative strategies that enhance overall cybersecurity posture, making networks more resilient to threats while emphasizing the need for thorough testing and validation of all software and hardware before going live.

Chapter 12: Case Studies of Supplier Assurance Failures

12.1 Analyzing Notable Breaches Due to Supplier Failures

Numerous high-profile breaches have underscored the risks associated with suppliers failing to meet cybersecurity standards. For instance, the Target data breach in 2013 showcased how the infiltration of a third-party vendor's system led to a massive compromise of customer data. Attackers gained access through an HVAC contractor, exploiting weak network segregation and outdated security practices. Similarly, in 2020, the SolarWinds hack highlighted the dangers posed when a supplier's software is compromised. The breach allowed malicious actors to infiltrate multiple U.S. federal agencies and private corporations via a widely used software update, emphasizing the profound impact that supplier vulnerabilities can have on downstream organizations. These incidents reveal not only the breaches' immediate effects but also the long-term trust issues they create between organizations and their customers.

Common trends observed in these incidents often involve a lack of stringent vetting processes for suppliers, inadequate communication of cybersecurity policies, and insufficient integration of security measures into the supply chain. Many organizations mistakenly prioritize cost and expedience over comprehensive security assessments. This approach can lead to overlooking essential factors such as compliance with industry standards, the financial stability of suppliers, and their commitment to ongoing security improvements. Additionally, there is often a noticeable absence of clear responsibilities and accountability when it comes to managing third-party risks. Organizations fail to adequately monitor their suppliers post-engagement, leaving gaps that vulnerabilities can exploit. As cyber threats evolve, a reactive rather than proactive stance only serves to exacerbate these issues.

To strengthen relationships with suppliers and mitigate risks, organizations must insist on a rigorous assurance route that includes not just initial assessments but ongoing evaluations of supplier security practices. Encouraging suppliers to undergo regular security audits and certifications—as well as implementing service-level agreements that clearly define security expectations—will establish a foundation of trust and accountability. Incorporating risk assessment protocols and requiring transparent reporting can further ensure that suppliers are not only chosen based on cost but also evaluated for their commitment to cybersecurity. Rigorous testing of code, software, and hardware before launch will help prevent breaches from taking hold, underscoring the importance of diligence in the supplier management process.

12.2 Lessons Learned from Cyber Security Incidents

Analyzing past supplier-related incidents reveals key lessons that can significantly enhance cyber security practices. Many breaches have originated due to inadequate vetting of suppliers, whose vulnerabilities become gateways for malicious actors. For instance, the Target breach exemplifies how third-party vendors can expose core networks by failing to secure their environments. A comprehensive understanding of such incidents emphasizes the necessity of a rigorous supplier assessment process. Organizations must scrutinize the security protocols of their vendors, ensuring they adhere to stringent compliance standards and are prepared to demonstrate their security measures. This ongoing vigilance can prevent breaches caused by weak links in the supply chain and fosters a culture of accountability across all partners involved in delivering products or services.

The importance of learning from failures cannot be overstated when it comes to strengthening cyber security practices. Incidents often serve as harsh teachers, revealing both strategic missteps and technical oversights. For example, organizations frequently overlook the critical need for proper incident response protocols or neglect the importance of routine security audits with their suppliers. Each failure highlights gaps that require immediate attention and remediation. Cyber security architects must proactively integrate lessons gleaned from past incidents into their assurance programs. This proactive stance not only aids in the reinforcement of existing measures but also fosters innovation in how organizations approach security. By establishing strong lines of communication and feedback with suppliers, businesses can bolster their defenses and ensure that both sides are aligned in the pursuit of robust security practices.

Ultimately, embracing lessons learned from past incidents requires a shift in mindset from reactive to proactive measures. Conducting thorough post-incident analyses can be extremely valuable. It is crucial to document not just what went wrong but also to identify what could have been done differently and implement those changes for the future. One practical tip for cyber security professionals is to establish an incident review board that includes stakeholders from various departments, including supplier management. This collaborative approach can yield insights that strengthen the overall cyber security posture. By continuously refining security strategies based on historical data and case studies, organizations can create a more secure ecosystem, both within their walls and throughout their supply chains.

12.3 Mitigating Future Risks through Case Analysis

Proactive strategies are essential for mitigating risks identified in various case studies. By examining past incidents, cybersecurity architects can develop foresight and implement defensive measures that address vulnerabilities before they can be exploited. A thorough analysis of case studies allows professionals to understand not just what went wrong but also why. This understanding facilitates the design of safeguards tailored to similar potential future threats. For instance, if a vulnerability was exploited due to inadequate supply chain security, organizations can create stricter vetting processes for suppliers, conduct regular audits, and use advanced tools for continuous monitoring. The goal is to anticipate what could go awry in their own systems and to adopt practices that preemptively counter these threats.

Adapting organizational practices based on historical data cannot be overstated. Utilizing lessons learned from previous breaches or security failures enables an organization to refine its operational protocols, ensuring they are ever-evolving in response to emerging threats. This includes reevaluating the effectiveness of security measures and adjusting them according to the insights gained from case analyses. Furthermore, it is crucial for cybersecurity professionals to foster a culture of learning within their teams, where past errors serve as case studies for future training sessions. This commitment to using historical data as a resource not only elevates the security posture of the organization but also instills confidence in stakeholders, including suppliers, by showcasing a proactive and informed approach to risk management.

To ensure that all components involving code, software, and hardware are rigorously tested before going live, organizations should implement a comprehensive assurance process. This process should encompass automated testing, peer reviews, and third-party audits to validate the security posture of applications and systems. Ensuring that every layer is examined through a lens of scrutiny mitigates the risk of known vulnerabilities being transferred into the live environment. Engaging with suppliers who adhere to these stringent testing protocols results in a fortified network, data integrity, and enhanced supply routes, promoting a robust cybersecurity framework across the entirety of the enterprise.

Chapter 13: Future Trends in Supplier Cyber Security Assurance

13.1 Evolving Threat Landscapes

The threat landscape is undergoing significant changes, largely influenced by advancements in technology and the increasing sophistication of cybercriminals. Suppliers, acting as crucial links in the supply chain, are often seen as vulnerable points that can be exploited by malicious actors. With the transition to cloud services, the rise of remote work, and the integration of the Internet of Things (IoT), organizations face new vulnerabilities. Cybersecurity professionals must be vigilant and recognize that traditional assurance methods may not suffice against threats that can now penetrate deeply into networks via suppliers. This demands a recalibrated approach, one that entails rigorous vetting of supplier security postures, continuous monitoring, and real-time threat intelligence sharing. As attackers develop more elaborate tactics, such as supply chain compromises and third-party exploitation, the scrutiny placed on supplier practices must intensify to safeguard organizational assets.

Alongside the shift in the threat landscape, several emerging threats are likely to reshape the field of cybersecurity assurance in the future. As artificial intelligence (AI) and machine learning technologies become more prevalent, they can be utilized both for enhancing security measures and for launching sophisticated attacks. Predictive algorithms may allow attackers to anticipate defensive actions, making it essential to embed security deep into the software development life cycle. Furthermore, the increasing trend toward automation can inadvertently introduce new vulnerabilities, as automated systems may lack the adaptability needed to respond to novel threats. The use of quantum computing also looms on the horizon, potentially rendering current encryption techniques obsolete. Cybersecurity professionals must remain proactive, understanding these trends and their potential implications on assurance practices, ensuring that suppliers adopt not only resilient technology but also an adaptive, forward-thinking security mindset.

This evolving landscape underscores the importance of maintaining continuous dialogue with suppliers. Adopting a model of shared responsibility for cybersecurity can enhance overall resilience. Practical steps such as implementing joint risk assessments, regular audits, and fostering transparency regarding vulnerabilities can significantly mitigate risks. Cybersecurity architects should advocate for the adoption of advanced assurances such as Software Bill of Materials (SBOMs) to track software components, ensuring that all third-party elements are scrutinized. The objective is not only to respond to threats as they arise but to create a comprehensive strategy that integrates supplier assurance into the broader organizational security framework.

13.2 Future Technologies Impacting Supplier Security

Innovative technologies are set to revolutionize supplier security by providing enhanced visibility, robustness, and resilience. The rise of Artificial Intelligence (AI) and Machine Learning (ML) allows organizations to analyze vast amounts of supplier data in real time, identifying anomalies or potential risks before they escalate. Blockchain technology is also proving to be transformative, offering a decentralized and immutable ledger that ensures the integrity of transactions, thus enhancing trust between suppliers and their partners. Moreover, the Internet of Things (IoT) enables greater connectivity and data exchange among devices and systems, facilitating more accurate assessments of supplier reliability and security posture. With the aid of advanced analytics, businesses can leverage predictive modeling to foresee potential supplier vulnerabilities, adjusting their strategies accordingly. Such proactive measures not only mitigate risks but also enhance compliance with regulatory frameworks that govern data security and privacy, making the supply chain more secure.

Integrating these new technologies into supplier management requires adaptive strategies that embrace agility and continuous improvement. Organizations should focus on developing a culture of collaboration with suppliers, fostering an environment where security practices are shared and enhanced through joint efforts. Establishing clear guidelines regarding the implementation of AI, blockchain, and IoT solutions can facilitate a smoother transition, allowing suppliers to align with security expectations. Regular training and upskilling programs focused on these technologies will also empower suppliers to adapt effectively to evolving threats. It is crucial to perform rigorous testing and validation of code, software, and hardware before going live, ensuring that each component of the supply chain can withstand potential cyber threats. By defining metrics for success and continuously measuring supplier performance against these criteria, companies can create a dynamic supplier ecosystem rooted in transparency and trust.

Additionally, organizations should consider investing in automated auditing tools that leverage AI to sort through and analyze vast datasets for compliance verification. This enables efficient identification of security gaps and fosters a culture of accountability among suppliers. Maintaining open lines of communication about security standards and expectations is equally essential. Cybersecurity professionals must regularly engage with suppliers to discuss emerging threats and share best practices, ensuring that both parties remain vigilant. By doing so, the organization can not only enhance its own security posture but also elevate the security standards of the entire supply chain, creating a secure network that thrives on innovation and resilience.

13.3 Preparing for Regulatory Changes

Anticipated regulatory changes are becoming increasingly significant in the realm of supplier cybersecurity. As governments and regulatory bodies around the world recognize the growing risks associated with cyber threats, they are stepping up efforts to establish stronger frameworks. Key areas of focus include data protection laws, breach notification requirements, and the integration of cybersecurity standards into procurement practices. Companies that rely on suppliers must be particularly vigilant, as non-compliance with these regulations not only affects the supplier but can also have direct implications for the organization's vulnerability to cyber risks. Suppliers of software, hardware, and critical services are being urged to enhance their cybersecurity measures. Regulations may require suppliers to implement comprehensive risk assessments, conduct regular security audits, and provide evidence of compliance. This shift demands that cybersecurity architects maintain a proactive stance in understanding these changes, adapting their strategies accordingly, and ensuring that suppliers demonstrate robust cybersecurity practices as part of their overall compliance obligations.

To adapt effectively to these new regulations, organizations should implement well-defined preparation strategies. Establishing a framework for ongoing communication with suppliers can facilitate a better understanding of regulatory expectations. Regular audits of supplier cybersecurity protocols can help in assessing compliance and identifying areas requiring improvement. It is essential to integrate compliance checks into the supplier management lifecycle, thus creating a culture of accountability. This may mean adopting tools and systems that allow for continuous monitoring and reporting on supplier security postures. Moreover, training programs should be instituted to educate supplier teams about regulatory requirements and the implications of non-compliance. Building strong alliances with legal and compliance teams can further enhance an organization's ability to respond swiftly to regulatory changes. By staying ahead of anticipated regulations and fostering transparent relationships with suppliers, cybersecurity professionals can better safeguard their networks, data, and supply chains. Leveraging compliance frameworks not only strengthens cybersecurity measures but also fosters trust between organizations and their suppliers.

One practical tip is to establish a regulatory change management team that focuses specifically on supplier compliance. This team can monitor emerging regulations and assess their potential impact on current supplier relationships, ensuring a smooth transition to new compliance demands and minimizing the risk of disruption. This dedicated approach allows for more agile responses to regulatory changes while bolstering the overall security posture of the organization.

Chapter 14: Developing a Supplier Assurance Framework

14.1 Framework Components and Best Practices

A comprehensive Supplier Assurance Framework is built upon several essential components that work together to ensure robust security and reliability. A thorough risk assessment is fundamental, as it allows organizations to evaluate the potential threats posed by suppliers and their impact on critical systems. This involves examining the security practices of suppliers, understanding their data handling processes, and assessing their compliance with relevant regulations and standards. Additionally, establishing clear contractual obligations regarding data protection, incident response, and information security helps define expectations and enhances accountability.

Another key component is the continuous monitoring and assessment of suppliers throughout the relationship. This means conducting regular audits and assessments, staying informed about any changes in the supplier's security posture, and ensuring that compliance measures are upheld over time. Utilizing automation tools can facilitate the monitoring process, making it easier to identify any deviations from agreed-upon standards. Training and awareness activities are also critical, ensuring that internal teams understand supplier risks and the importance of adhering to the established framework.

Best practices for implementing and executing a Supplier Assurance Framework involve a proactive and iterative approach. It is vital to engage suppliers early in the process, fostering collaboration and transparency to ensure mutual understanding of security expectations. Regular communication helps maintain alignment and can uncover potential issues before they escalate. Furthermore, organizations should invest in developing standardized assessment tools and frameworks that can be readily applied to different suppliers, promoting consistency and efficiency in the evaluation process. Documenting all interactions, assessments, and changes to the framework allows businesses to create a historical record that can serve as a basis for refining processes and improving overall supplier security practices.

Ultimately, ensuring that suppliers adhere to rigorous testing before any code, software, or hardware goes live is crucial. Establishing a clear testing protocol, inclusive of automated testing methods, vulnerability scanning, and real-world scenario evaluations, significantly mitigates the risks associated with compromise. By fostering a culture of accountability and transparency, organizations enhance their resilience against supply chain threats, ensuring that their networks and data remain secure against evolving cyber threats.

14.2 Establishing Governance Structures

Effective supplier management requires a well-defined governance structure that aligns with organizational goals while addressing cybersecurity risks. To establish this structure, organizations should start by identifying key roles that will oversee supplier activities, ensuring there is clarity in accountability. This includes creating specific committees or boards focused on supplier performance, risks, and compliance. Governance structures should encompass a series of policies and procedures that dictate how suppliers are evaluated, selected, and monitored. Setting these frameworks helps maintain the integrity of the supplier relationship and serves as a safety net against potential cybersecurity threats.

Clearly defining the criteria for performance assessments ensures that suppliers adhere to required security standards, facilitating ongoing compliance and reducing vulnerabilities that could affect the organization's data and network. Furthermore, the governance structure must allow for agility in adapting to changes in the threat landscape, establishing protocols for regular assessment and integration of novel security measures aimed at fostering robust supplier assurance.

The roles of various stakeholders in the supplier assurance process are crucial for the holistic success of cybersecurity management. Cybersecurity professionals need to collaborate with procurement, legal, and operational teams to ensure a comprehensive approach that covers all aspects of supplier interactions. Procurement teams are instrumental in vendor selection, requiring cybersecurity professionals to provide input on security capabilities and risk assessments for potential suppliers. Legal departments will play a vital role in drafting contracts that include strict compliance clauses relating to cybersecurity, thereby making sure the supplier's obligations are clearly outlined. Operational teams are responsible for integrating suppliers into everyday business processes and ensuring they adhere to security protocols during daily operations. By maintaining a cohesive network of stakeholders, organizations enhance communication and foster a culture of security that permeates throughout the supplier assurance process. Regular meetings and updates among these stakeholders can help identify and mitigate risks before they escalate into significant threats.

One of the most crucial aspects of establishing effective governance structures is the commitment to continuous improvement and scrutiny of security practices across the supply chain. Adopt a strategy that includes regular audits and performance reviews, combining both subjective evaluations and objective metrics. This approach will not only help identify gaps in the current supplier assurance processes but also adjust to the prevalence of emerging threats. Investing in training opportunities tailored for stakeholders involved in supplier management can elevate the overall security posture of the organization. By ensuring that everyone is on the same page regarding security expectations and practices, organizations can significantly enhance their resilience against unforeseen cybersecurity incidents that could emerge from weak supplier engagement.

14.3 Continuous Improvement Processes

Continuous improvement processes are critical for maintaining supplier assurance, especially in the context of cyber security. The principles of continuous improvement rest on the belief that even small, incremental enhancements can lead to significant advancements over time. It is essential for cyber security professionals to work closely with suppliers to ensure they adhere to robust assurance practices. This can be achieved through regular communication, establishing clear expectations, and fostering a culture that prioritizes quality and security. By integrating these principles, organizations can create a resilient framework that adapts to evolving threats and strengthens their defense against potential vulnerabilities that may arise from the supply chain.

The mechanisms for regularly reviewing and enhancing assurance practices involve systematic assessments and evaluations. Establishing metrics for success, such as vulnerability detection rates and incident response times, provides valuable insight into the effectiveness of current practices. Regular audits should be scheduled to identify areas that require improvement, ensuring that these assessments are tailored to the specific risks faced by the organization and its suppliers. Feedback loops, where information gathered from testing and monitoring activities informs the enhancement of policies and procedures, create an environment of continuous learning. Leveraging automated tools and data analytics can also help streamline this process, enabling real-time adjustments in response to emerging threats and ensuring that suppliers maintain a high standard of security before their products and services go live.

Incorporating feedback from both internal and external stakeholders during these reviews is essential for refining assurance practices. Engaging team members, suppliers, and even customers can lead to diverse insights that drive innovation and enhance security measures. Emphasizing a proactive stance in testing code, software, and hardware increases confidence in the supplier's ability to meet rigorous security standards. By establishing a framework for continuous learning and improvement, organizations not only enhance their security posture but also cultivate stronger relationships with suppliers, creating a collaborative approach to security that reaps benefits for all parties involved.

Chapter 15: Conclusion and Next Steps

15.1 Key Takeaways from the Book

This book has provided crucial insights into the intricate world of cybersecurity, particularly emphasizing the importance of a comprehensive assurance framework when working with suppliers. One of the most critical takeaways is the necessity for cybersecurity professionals to adopt a proactive stance in their engagements with third-party vendors. As threats become increasingly sophisticated, relying on outdated assumptions about supplier security can expose organizations to significant risks. Key lessons include the need for thorough assessments of vendor security protocols, the establishment of transparent communication channels, and the fostering of collaborative relationships where cybersecurity practices are consistently scrutinized and improved. The significance of continuous monitoring and evaluation cannot be overstated; the dynamic nature of cyber threats requires that assurance doesn't end with the initial vetting but is an ongoing process. Understanding the full scope of potential vulnerabilities tied to suppliers is essential for maintaining robust organizational security.

Encouraging cybersecurity professionals to prioritize supplier assurance is a vital part of establishing a resilient security posture. It is imperative to recognize that suppliers are an extension of the organization's own security landscape. Engaging in rigorous testing and validation of both code and hardware before deployment not only safeguards the organization's data but also reinforces trust with clients and stakeholders. Cybersecurity professionals must advocate for and implement rigorous supplier audits, ensuring that all supply routes and data interactions are secure and reliable. By prioritizing supplier accountability, organizations can create a more fortified network where the integrity of all components is assured, significantly mitigating the risk of data breaches and cyber-attacks. Working closely with suppliers to ensure they adhere to best practices in cybersecurity will yield dividends in the form of enhanced protection and operational resilience.

As a practical tip, consider implementing a supplier risk management framework that includes regular assessments, clear performance metrics, and a strong incident response collaboration initiative. This hands-on approach will ensure that you stay ahead of potential vulnerabilities and foster an environment of shared responsibility in securing your network.

15.2 Establishing Next Steps for Implementation

Implementing supplier assurance initiatives requires a clear and actionable strategy. Start by conducting thorough assessments of your suppliers' cybersecurity processes to identify vulnerabilities and strengths. This can involve requesting detailed documentation regarding their security practices, including protocols for data protection, incident response strategies, and compliance with relevant regulations. Engage in regular discussions to ensure that these suppliers understand your organization's security requirements and expectations. Create a checklist that reflects your specific needs, which can be used during supplier evaluations. This checklist can help clarify the areas that require deeper scrutiny, such as the methods used for testing code and software before deployment.

To foster accountability throughout the implementation process, establish realistic timelines that account for both your own organizational workload and your suppliers' capacities. It is essential to collaborate closely with them, setting measurable milestones along the way. This collaborative approach not only enhances trust but also ensures that everyone maintains a clear focus on progress. Utilize project management tools to keep everyone on track, allowing for real-time updates and transparency regarding responsibilities. Assign specific individuals to oversee each aspect of the supplier assurance process, making sure everyone knows who is responsible for what, which strengthens accountability.

Monitoring progress should not be overlooked, as this is key to ensuring that the assurance processes remain effective. Schedule regular checkpoints to review adherence to established security practices and ensure that any identified risks are being adequately addressed. Continuous feedback loops between your team and suppliers can help in fine-tuning the assurance processes, enhancing the overall security posture. Remember, fostering a culture of communication and collaboration is vital to this initiative's success, creating a shared understanding of the importance of cybersecurity. A handy tip is to document everything from the initial assessments through to the feedback provided during the project. This not only creates a history to refer back to but can also be useful for regulatory compliance and future negotiations.

15.3 The Importance of Ongoing Supplier Engagement

Continuous engagement with suppliers is crucial in the realm of cybersecurity. Cyber threats evolve rapidly, and suppliers play a significant role in an organization's overall security posture. By maintaining an ongoing dialogue with suppliers, cybersecurity professionals can ensure that they are aware of the latest vulnerabilities and threats associated with the products and services they provide. This relationship allows for shared best practices around security measures and helps to cultivate a proactive stance in identifying potential issues before they escalate into serious compromises. Regular check-ins, discussions on threat intelligence, and updates on software patches and hardware upgrades can facilitate a more robust security framework. When cybersecurity architects prioritize supplier relationships, they not only strengthen their defenses but also build a synergistic partnership that enhances the overall resilience of their networks and data systems.

Adaptive strategies are essential to maintaining assurance over time as the threat landscape shifts. Cybersecurity professionals must develop flexible frameworks that enable quick adjustments to security protocols in response to new information and emerging threats. Engaging suppliers in this process ensures that both parties are aligned on risk management approaches and adaptive strategies. This means establishing clear communication channels where changes in security practices can be discussed openly and incorporating supplier feedback into decision-making processes. With frequent updates and an open line of communication, organizations can tailor their security frameworks to the unique needs of their suppliers while also ensuring these partners meet the necessary compliance and testing standards. By fostering an environment of collaboration, organizations can enhance their security posture through adaptive strategies that not only react to threats but anticipate and mitigate them before they affect operations.

In the cybersecurity domain, testing of code, software, and hardware is indispensable before any solution goes live. It is essential to establish thorough vetting processes that suppliers must adhere to, ensuring that their offerings have undergone rigorous testing. Continuous engagement allows cybersecurity professionals to understand suppliers' testing methods and the resources they dedicate to quality assurance. This mutual understanding fosters a culture of accountability where both the organization and the supplier share the burden of cybersecurity. It is advisable to implement regular reviews of supplier testing protocols and involve them in joint assessments of the risks associated with their products. Building these practices into the supplier engagement process not only enhances trust but also solidifies the integrity of the entire supply chain.